THE PATH TO PURPOSE

RYAN DENISON, PhD
AND JIM DENISON, PhD

Also from Denison Forum

The Daily Article email newsletter is news discerned differently every Monday through Friday.
Subscribe for free at DenisonForum.org.

The Fifth Great Awakening and the Future of America

How Does God See America?

What Are My Spiritual Gifts?

*A Light Unto My Path:
A Practical Guide to Studying the Bible*

*How to Bless God by Blessing Others:
Words of Wisdom from the Early Church
to Christians Today*

*The Coming Tsunami: Why Christians Are Labeled
Intolerant, Irrelevant, Oppressive, and Dangerous—and
How We Can Turn the Tide*

Biblical Insight to Tough Questions: Vols. 1–11

*Every Hour I Need Thee:
A Practical Guide to Daily Prayer*

Request these books and more at
DenisonForum.org/store

THE PATH TO PURPOSE

RYAN DENISON, PhD
AND JIM DENISON, PhD

© 2023 Denison Forum

Unless otherwise indicated, all Scripture quotations are from the ESV® Bible (The Holy Bible, English Standard Version®), copyright © 2001 by Crossway, a publishing ministry of Good News Publishers. Used by permission. All rights reserved.

Scripture quotations marked MSG are taken from The Message, copyright © 1993, 2002, 2018 by Eugene H. Peterson. Used by permission of NavPress. All rights reserved. Represented by Tyndale House Publishers.

Table of Contents

The life to which we're called (Mt 5:1–16) 1

Christ's standards for discipleship (Mt 5:17–20) 13

Stop pretending (Mt 5:21–32) 21

Prioritize your witness (Mt 5:33–48) 35

Serve secretly (Mt 6:1–24) 49

Worry not (Mt 6:25–7:11) 63

Build on the rock (Mt 7:12–27) 77

Recognize God's authority (Mt 7:28–29) 91

Appendix: A brief summary of the Beatitudes 95

About the Authors 97

About Denison Ministries 98

1

The life to which we're called

Matthew 5:1–16

A primary emphasis in Matthew's gospel is helping Christians learn how to be better followers of Christ while guiding others to do the same. To that end, he bookends Jesus' teaching ministry with two passages that work to that effect: the Sermon on the Mount and the Great Commission. The God who inspired Matthew's writing was clearly concerned with making sure that his people remembered Jesus came to accomplish far more than just securing our eternal salvation.

The day we trust Christ as our savior and Lord is the start of a relationship that will extend throughout all of eternity. Too often, though, we make the mistake of thinking that eternity doesn't start until we get to heaven. The truth is that we are called to invest in that relationship in this life as well as in the life to come, and that means becoming more like Christ every single day.

So what does that look like?

THE PATH TO PURPOSE

It has often been said that Christians are meant to represent God's hands and feet to the world around us. Yet that mission is doomed to fail if we cannot represent his heart and mind as well. The religious leaders in the time of Christ perfected how to serve God from a fallen, human point of view. They placed the utmost importance on the observance of his laws and created safeguard upon safeguard to ensure that people would not transgress them.

The Gospels, however, are filled with examples of how God incarnate desires more from his people. Fortunately, he also left us with a clear guide on how to serve him with our hearts and minds as well as with our actions.

In the Sermon on the Mount, Jesus essentially gives us his systematic ethic for how to be his disciples. Valid arguments can be made whether the Sermon was given all at once or if it's a summary of his teachings. But that issue is ultimately irrelevant to the Sermon's meaning and importance.

Either way, the Sermon on the Mount represents the core of what Jesus spent three years telling people across the Jewish world. It covers a wide range of topics that encompass most every facet of what he expects of those who claim to follow him. As St. Augustine describes, the Sermon represents "a perfect standard of the Christian life."

To that end, it's fitting that the Sermon is also how Matthew chose to start his account of the teaching portion of Christ's ministry. He wanted his readers to see it as the lens through which we should understand the rest of Christ's teachings and to note that it lays the foundation for understanding all that comes afterward.

Given the gravity of what's to follow, however, it must have come as a shock when Jesus began by stating, "Blessed are the poor in spirit, for theirs is the kingdom of heaven." When he continued on with a series of seven additional blessings, all of which were countercultural to the society of his day (and ours as well), it would have been impossible to avoid coming to the same conclusion as that of the crowds who first heard him: this man is different from the rest of our teachers (Matthew 7:29).

You see, contrary to the way in which the law was presented by most religious leaders of his time, Jesus began his instruction on how to live with a focus on character rather than commands. And until we understand why, we'll never fully grasp the gravity of all the instruction that comes after.

Even if we somehow managed to keep every command found in this sermon but did not exhibit the characteristics described in its first twelve verses, then we would never fully experience the blessing of God in our lives. Nor would we become the salt and light our culture needs.

So, with that purpose in mind, what makes these Beatitudes (taken from the Latin phrase for blessings) so important? After all, the Scriptures are filled with teachings on the kind of character God wants to see in his people, so why highlight these specific traits?

Those questions are explored in greater depth in our book on the Beatitudes: *Blessed: Eight Ways Christians Change Culture*, and you can find a brief summary of each Beatitude in the appendix at the end of this book. A few thoughts are worth noting here as well, though.

"Blessed are the . . . ."

To begin, we must note how Jesus states each Beatitude. While I doubt many will read this book hoping for a grammar lesson (I know I wouldn't), a few key pieces of information are vital if we want to understand fully all that Christ says in these verses.

First, Jesus offers us a guide to the kinds of blessings only God can provide.

It's a blessedness that transcends our circumstances, a joy and peace the world can neither give nor take. From the start, we must acknowledge that what the Lord offers is something only he can provide.

Second, Jesus says, "Blessed *are* . . . ."

Not "blessed were" when times were better or "blessed will be" when your current troubles pass, but "blessed are" because the blessings God uniquely offers are available to you each and every moment of your life. Those who live with the character described in these verses will know and abide in a kind of blessing that too often we mistakenly believe is reserved for heaven (or, at least, our more peaceful times on earth).

Third, Jesus states, "Blessed are *the* . . . ."

In seven of the eight Beatitudes, Jesus begins by using some form of that definitive article to describe those who are blessed, with the only exception being when he personalizes those who are persecuted in the final Beatitude. By starting with some variation of "blessed are *the/those*," Jesus demonstrates that these characteristics form the only path to the blessing God wants us to have.

There is no other way because there could not be another way. The remnants of our fallen nature simply make it too difficult to otherwise live every day with the kind of character Jesus describes in these verses.

So, we've seen that Jesus was emphatic about both the uniqueness and the necessity of these characteristics for those who want to experience the kind of blessing only God can provide. But are all of them necessary? Can we experience enough blessing to get by and live out the kind of obedience he prescribes in the rest of the Sermon if we just focus on the few that come easiest to us?

A systematic ethic

It's human nature to gravitate toward that which can make us feel less overwhelmed. And it's an inherently overwhelming task to conform our character to each of the traits espoused in the Beatitudes. But we must not focus on following the Beatitudes that come more naturally to us while ignoring those that require more effort on our part. Jesus did not intend to give us that option.

When Christ began by stating, "Blessed are the poor in spirit, for theirs is the kingdom of heaven," he laid the foundation upon which the other Beatitudes would be built. The same general principle is true of all the Beatitudes. Each of them describes a component of the Christian life without which our character will fall short of the standard to which Jesus has called us.

Moreover, we cannot consistently practice some of these traits to the exclusion of the rest.

- Those who mourn can only be comforted if they are poor in spirit and therefore open to the kingship of Christ in their lives.

- The pure in heart will see God because they hunger and thirst for righteousness with a meekness that has enabled them to entrust every facet of their lives to the Father.

- And those who are persecuted for righteousness' sake can find the strength to rejoice and be glad because they have learned to see themselves as members of God's kingdom and, more importantly, his family.

Such examples could be given for each of the Beatitudes, and it is vital that we approach this section of God's word convinced of the absolute necessity of every characteristic Jesus chose to include. The Beatitudes truly form a systematic ethic for what it means to be a disciple of Christ. Absent that holistic approach, we cannot fully appreciate the kind of life to which we are called.

But what does that life look like?

The nature of blessing

As we've seen, living in accordance with the characteristics described in the Beatitudes is necessary for positioning ourselves to receive the blessings Christ promises and to be equipped to obey the commands that follow in the rest of the Sermon. Yet, to fully appreciate what that means, a brief word must first be said as to the nature of these blessings.

After all, the same Jesus who made these promises also guaranteed that we would encounter trouble and persecution, so he could not have had in mind a life free of struggle.

In truth, being blessed as he describes in these verses is not essential to living a good, happy life. At times, it can even seem counterproductive to those aims. Such a life simply wasn't what Christ most desired for his followers. Rather, what he promised was a life of purpose and fulfillment, an existence in which we can genuinely feel as though we're making a difference.

In short, what the Beatitudes promise and the Sermon as a whole prescribes are the necessary blessings to be a force for the kingdom in the world around us. If we're honest with ourselves, isn't that what we really crave most?

We can momentarily satiate our desire for happiness and peace in any number of ways, many of which are neither wicked nor sinful. Yet, when that brief joy fades, the gnawing for something more, for the kind of life Jesus describes in these verses, will always return. The only way to end that cycle is to devote our lives so completely to the Lord and his ways that every moment is saturated with his presence.

Fortunately, that's exactly what the Beatitudes are meant to accomplish. They are, in a sense, Christ's vision for what our lives could be like if we let him be our king. It is not a life of ease, and it will require the kind of self-sacrifice that does not come naturally to us. It is, however, the only way to know the kind of lasting joy and purpose for which we were created. And it is the only way to be the salt and light that will change our culture for God's glory.

Salt and light

As countercultural principles that are difficult for us to live out on any given day, the Beatitudes would seem much easier to keep if we separated ourselves from the world.

Christians have tried that from time to time across the years. Monasteries, for example, started in large part as a way for a select group of Christians to live out their faith in theoretical safety from the temptations and harsher elements of life that made it difficult for the masses to follow Jesus devoutly. Part of their job was to preserve the faith for everyone else.

That purpose still has a place in Christ's calling to his disciples. A primary purpose of salt in the ancient world was to preserve food and keep it from going bad. In a time when there was no electricity and refrigeration of any sort was often impossible, the most common way to keep meat from spoiling was to cure it with salt. As such, a key element of Jesus identifying us as "salt of the earth" (Matthew 5:13) is the idea that we are meant to preserve what's good and protect it from the degrading influences around us.

It's important to note, though, that we are not called "salt of the faith" or "salt of the religion." Christ's call is not to preserve the church or Christianity—he doesn't need our help for that—but rather the world, and we can't do that in isolation from the world.

Going back to the example of the monasteries, that movement's most enduring legacy often had less to do with preserving the faith than taking the most devoted followers of Christ and removing them from the general public. To use Christ's next metaphor, one might say they hid their light under a bowl and the world around them often suffered as a result (v. 15).

There are some today who look at the state of the culture around us and argue that Christians should do something similar: we should mostly withdraw from the larger society to protect our faith until a time when the world is more receptive to it. The temptation to do so is understandable.

Jesus, however, was clear that we have been called to a different kind of life—one lived in the world but not of the world, as Billy Graham put it.

Eugene Peterson described this life well in his translation of these verses:

> Let me tell you why you are here. You're here to be salt-seasoning that brings out the God-flavors of this earth. If you lose your saltiness, how will people taste godliness? You've lost your usefulness and will end up in the garbage. Here's another way to put it: You're here to be light, bringing out the God-colors in the world. God is not a secret to be kept. We're going public with this, as public as a city on a hill. If I make you light-bearers, you don't think I'm going to hide you under a bucket, do you? I'm putting you on a light stand. Now that I've put you there on a hilltop, on a light stand—shine! Keep open house; be generous with your lives. By opening up to others, you'll prompt people to open up with God, this generous Father in heaven. (Matthew 5:13–16, MSG)

Prompting "people to open up with God" is the primary purpose of every Christian life. Verse 16 makes clear that Jesus calls his disciples to be salt and light in order to point people back to the Father. And, as we will see across the following chapters, it is impossible to be fully obedient to the Lord in either character or action if our focus strays from bringing him glory.

But if we are to accomplish this purpose effectively, it will require a daily commitment to a lifestyle defined by heaven's standards rather than our own. In short, it requires a Beatitudes approach to life.

The irony is that it's only by living in a way that runs counter to our fallen natures that we can become what Jesus says we already are.

Remember, he told his followers: you are the salt of the earth and you are the light of the world. These are not descriptions of what they might one day become but rather inherent, present-tense characteristics of their identity as his disciples.

As countercultural as a Beatitudes way of life may seem, it is exactly who God created us to be and exactly what our culture desperately needs us to be.

So what does that look like?

We've seen what it means for the character Christ wants to develop in us, but how does it impact the way we act around others?

In what ways does it change our approach to the larger world around us?

And how does it alter the standards to which our heavenly Father holds his children?

As we'll soon see, those questions comprise the focus of the Sermon's remaining passages and give us some guidance on how to practically live out the virtues Jesus espoused in these first sixteen verses.

To that end, he continued by clarifying the righteousness to which we are called by contrasting it with the righteousness of the scribes and Pharisees—the subject of the next chapter.

2

Christ's standards for discipleship

Matthew 5:17–20

To this point in the Sermon on the Mount, Jesus had introduced several radically new ways of thinking about one's relationship with God and the responsibilities such a relationship entailed. He'd redefined the nature of what it means to be blessed by God, called his disciples to be public examples of a kind of devotion that stood in stark contrast to the way religion was most often practiced in his day, and was about to spend the rest of the Sermon going even farther in that direction.

But, before continuing down that path, he paused for a moment to make it very clear that though his teachings may seem new, they are in no way counter to the Law and the Prophets. In fact, they are the fulfillment and highest understanding of those core pillars of Jewish life, a claim that would have been just as radical as anything he had said up to this point. The terminology that Jesus used to describe what he came to fulfill is crucial to understanding this task.

The Pharisees had good intentions but still erred

You see, the Law and the Prophets encompassed the whole of Jewish Scripture at this point—our Old Testament. It was the entirety of God's revelatory word to his people. However, it was not the whole of what most Jews considered to be important or sacred, and that was especially true for the scribes and Pharisees to whom Jesus alludes in Matthew 5:20.

In addition to the written Law and the teachings of the Prophets, Jewish leaders had slowly built up a set of oral laws intended to help ensure that God's people did not stray outside of his will and break any of the written commandments. By the time of Jesus, there were more than six hundred such rules.

Many of these came less from the Lord's direction than from human attempts to try to help people keep the fundamental tenets of God's will. For the scribes and Pharisees, however, the oral laws were often seen as equally inviolable to anything written in the Scriptures themselves.

Unfortunately, instead of helping people draw closer to the Lord, these laws instead created a system of works righteousness that led people farther away from him. They encouraged a transactional sort of relationship that runs counter to the life God wants to have with us.

So Jesus, having come to reestablish the kind of relationship with the Lord for which we were created, knew that he'd have to correct that mistake before we could know the Father as he wants to be known.

To that end, he purposefully set about breaking many of these man-made commandments—particularly those related to the Sabbath—over the course of his ministry. In many ways, he *had* come to abolish these laws, and he would do so by helping people better understand the Law and the Prophets, as well as how to apply them correctly.

But before we move on to look more closely at the righteousness to which we are called in these verses, it's important to note that—for the most part—the religious leaders enforced these rules with the best of intentions. They earnestly desired to understand the Law and obey it in every facet of their lives. And they wanted to help others do the same.

They did not set out to become the religious police. They were just so afraid of seeing Israel go back to the kind of rebellious disregard for the Lord that had gotten them exiled that they went too far in the opposite direction. In short, they were so caught up in following God's laws that they forgot to include him in the conversation.

The gravity of their mistakes is perhaps best illustrated by the fact that Jesus took the totality of their laws—both those from oral tradition and God's written word—and condensed them into two basic principles: Love the Lord your God with all your heart, soul, strength, and mind, and love your neighbor as yourself (Luke 10:27).

We easily recognize the errors of the scribes and Pharisees today because we have the benefit of people pointing them out for the better part of two thousand years. People are still prone to make the same mistake today, though. None of us is immune to the temptation of attempting to serve God without asking God how he wants to be served.

And, if we fail to recognize that flaw in ourselves, then we're likely to turn Christ's teachings in the remainder of the sermon into the same kinds of stiff regulations our Lord was trying to correct.

So how can we avoid making that mistake?

What we have to understand

Christ's solution to the kind of self-guided attempts at righteousness we see with the religious leaders was to return to Scripture, but to do so on God's terms.

Matthew 5:18 makes clear that "not an iota, not a dot, will pass from the Law until all is accomplished." And he doubled down on that sentiment in the following verse where he warns that "whoever relaxes one of the least of these commandments and teaches others to do the same will be called least in the kingdom of heaven."

Jesus' plan for helping people understand and embrace a God-centered righteousness was not going to be found by disregarding God's laws. But those laws were never intended to be sufficient to grant the righteousness that the Lord desires.

Rather, as Paul points out "if a law had been given that could give life, then righteousness would indeed be by the law. But the Scripture imprisoned everything under sin, so that the promise by faith in Jesus Christ might be given to those who believe. Now before faith came, we were held captive under the law, imprisoned until the coming faith would be revealed. So then, the law was our guardian until Christ came, in order that we might be justified by faith" (Galatians 3:21–24).

It's human nature to want to save ourselves. We see that basic fact at work from the time when Adam and Eve believed Satan's first lie to the development of most every religion that exists outside of the Judeo-Christian faith. However, the belief that there is something we can do to merit God's salvation and justify ourselves before the Lord will always prevent us from embracing the only kind of faith that is truly able to save.

Jesus wanted to make sure that his disciples and the crowds gathered around them understood that such faith requires an understanding of our own weakness. When we relax the truth of God's word to make it more accommodating to others or twist our interpretation in order to disregard the parts we don't like, then it becomes more difficult to fully appreciate our need for the Lord.

And, given the value much of our culture currently places on toleration and personal truth, this need to reckon with our own fallenness will be one of the primary ways in which a right understanding of our faith comes into conflict with what we're likely to hear from the lost around us. It's also one of the reasons that so many have trouble coming to Christ.

After all, a 2021 survey showed that nearly 40 percent of Americans—including 45 percent of Christians—believe that a person does not even need to believe in God to go to heaven, much less have a personal, saving relationship with Jesus. The gap between people's awareness of their need for God and the reality of that need is staggering, but it's also likely to continue growing across the coming years. And when God's people relax God's commandments, we exacerbate the problem.

That urgency does not mean, however, that we should go back to the legalistic, hellfire-and-brimstone damnation that so often defined people's perception of the faith in recent decades.

As we'll see across the following chapters, that kind of fear-based relationship with the Father is not what Jesus prescribes. Rather, the purpose of the Law is to drive home how utterly lost and without hope we are apart from God's intervention.

At the same time, though, Jesus is also clear that whoever does keep these commandments and helps others to do the same "will be called great in the kingdom of heaven" (Matthew 5:19). Consequently, it seems clear that there is more to the role of the Law and the prophets than simply reminding people of their sin.

So what is that second role, and how does it relate to the kind of righteousness Jesus encourages his followers to pursue?

Why does the Law exist?

The religious leaders were acutely aware of their fellow countrymen's inability to keep every "iota" and "dot" of the Law. In that sense, they got the first half of the Lord's plan for salvation right.

The problem was that their solution was simply to try harder, so they created more rules rather than allow that awareness to drive them into a greater dependence on the Lord. That's why Jesus states in verse 20 that "unless your righteousness exceeds that of the scribes and Pharisees, you will never enter the kingdom of heaven."

Our Lord made this startling statement to emphasize just how impossible it was to save oneself and to encourage his followers not to try.

You see, the religious leaders had become so strict with keeping the letter of the law that they'd set up a system that actually incentivized finding ways to relax it. Adhering to every facet of God's rules was of such vital importance that they had to try to make that goal manageable. To that end, the hundreds of additional laws they created in order to safeguard God's Law often placed the greatest emphasis on the minute, insignificant parts that were ultimately attainable through human effort. And, in so doing, they fundamentally altered the purpose of the Law within Jewish society.

If we think back to the Exodus and the context in which the Law was first given to the Hebrews, it was meant to help them understand their identity as God's people. They had been slaves in Egypt for the better part of four centuries, and that had become the defining principle in how they understood their existence. Though they had longed for liberation, that freedom removed a core tenet of how they saw themselves. The fact that they often yearned to go back to slavery when times got tough demonstrates just how strong a role this history continued to play in their mindset, especially for that first generation (Numbers 14:4).

As such, the Law was intended to give them a new foundation for their identity in God—one that could help them focus every facet of their lives on the Lord. And that relationship is the prerequisite for keeping the Law because it's the only way that the Law can fulfill its true purpose. If every "iota" and "dot" are not drawing us closer to God, then it doesn't matter how closely they are kept.

While we may not hold to every facet of the Law today in the same way the Israelites did, the basic purpose of God's commands has not changed. We have been given a new identity in Christ, but Jesus makes clear that our new identity is not divorced from the moral obligations to which he alludes in these verses, as well as those that follow.

Obedience to God and the intense desire to follow his will—a hunger and thirst for righteousness, to put it in the terms he uses in verse 6—remain foundational to what it means to be his disciples. And if we want to be "called great in the kingdom of heaven," then we need to place as much importance on pursuing that righteousness as he does.

Again, though, we must remember that such a pursuit is fruitless unless it draws us closer to him. Moreover, as will become clear as Christ unpacks the true meaning of that righteousness across the rest of the sermon, that pursuit is ultimately impossible without the Lord's help.

And that's the point.

So as we transition now into a closer look at some of the ways in which Christ's understanding of the Law diverges from the self-righteousness practiced by the religious leaders, remember that it's all right if these standards seem impossibly high—because they are. The inevitability of our failure, however, is not a reason for discouragement or for relaxing God's standards. Rather, it's meant to serve as a constant reminder of our need for the Lord and to keep us walking close to him.

To that end, Jesus continues to unpack the true meaning of the Law and the prophets by calling us to address the sin in our hearts rather than focusing first on its outward manifestations.

3

Stop pretending

Matthew 5:21–32
(anger, lust, divorce)

The passage we discussed in the previous chapter serves as a hinge of sorts that takes the Sermon from Christ's introduction, in which he laid out the character and purpose of being his disciple, and pivots to the practical application of those principles in everyday life.

Laying that foundation was important because we have no hope of obeying the commands that follow unless our hearts and minds are in obedience to his will. Jesus demonstrates this fact by starting this second part of his Sermon with a series of six statements that circumvent the traditional understanding of morality.

In these verses, Jesus moves away from an emphasis on one's actions—the traditional approach to combatting sin in his culture—to focus instead on the motivation behind those actions.

And he begins each of those statements with some variation of "You have heard that it was said . . . . But I say to you" in order to remove any remaining doubt that his approach will differ from what his audience was accustomed to hearing.

As he established only a few verses before, however, this seemingly unique approach is not in any way counter to a true understanding of the Law and the Prophets. Remembering that the commands that follow, both in these six statements and the rest of the sermon, are not new (even if they seem novel) is crucial to gaining an accurate understanding of what the Lord expects of his disciples.

The standards Jesus describes have always been God's standards for his people. We just haven't always accepted the challenge of living up to them. And, as we'll see with each of these six examples, the reason why we often struggle to meet these standards goes back to the issue of where our focus lies.

God wants more from us than being a people focused on following the rules. He wants a people who truly desire to know him better and who follow his will out of love rather than obligation. When we understand the principles behind God's commands, we are better enabled to follow them and apply them to every situation.

Essentially, when we are not so obsessed with ensuring we obey every law, we can better learn how to trust God's guidance from moment to moment. That reliance on the Lord will, in turn, lead to a much deeper and more fruitful relationship with our heavenly Father. Ironically, it is also the best way to make sure we're keeping his commands as well.

But before we look at some of those commands more closely, here's why we separated this passage as we did.

While the basic format of each statement in this passage is similar, the sins addressed fall into two main categories: private and public.

Anger, lust, and divorce—the three addressed below—are more private in nature. As we will see when we examine each, these sins often manifest initially in ways that are difficult for others to recognize. While, if left unchecked, they can eventually result in outward action, we can harbor them in our hearts in ways that often go unnoticed to all but the Lord. Moreover, these are also sins most people tend to recognize we should not commit. As a result, we are more inclined to hide their manifestations where possible.

The second group (oaths, retaliation, and loving your enemies) is more public in nature. They often deal more with how we treat others and can be easier to justify in the eyes of those who commit them, meaning we are often less inclined to hide them.

So, with that context in mind, we will examine the first three of those statements in this chapter and the next three in chapter 4.

Anger

The first issue Jesus addresses in this section of his sermon is anger. He begins by stating: "You have heard that it was said to those of old, 'You shall not murder; and whoever murders will be liable to judgment.' But I say to you that everyone who is angry with his brother will be liable to judgment; whoever insults his brother will be liable to the council; and whoever says, 'You fool!' will be liable to the hell of fire" (Matthew 5:21–22).

An important distinction is lost, however, when we read this verse in English. You see, two words in the Greek are often translated as anger. The first, *thumos*, most commonly refers to the spontaneous emotion. This kind of anger is what we feel when someone wrongs us or when circumstances don't go our way, and it is not what Jesus calls a sin in this passage. After all, even Jesus experienced the emotion of anger—such as when he drove out the money changers (Matthew 21:12–13)—yet was without sin.

That Christ does not condemn the emotion of anger reveals an important principle for understanding both this statement and the ones that follow: the Bible does not tell us how to feel, only how to respond to those feelings. In the next chapter, for example, we will take a look at Jesus' command to love our enemies. He can command us to love because love is not an emotion; it's a choice. As a result, we have some measure of control over whether or not we will love another person.

In the same way, Christ can warn against anger in these verses because he is not talking about the initial emotion but rather what we choose to do with it.

The word he uses in verse 22 to describe this anger is *orgizomenos*, a verb perhaps better translated as something akin to holding a grudge. It's an anger that is cherished in the heart, nursed and kept alive by our own volition. This kind of anger is a choice and, as such, a sin that is within our power to avoid.

If our focus, however, remains fixed on the outward displays of anger that are more commonly associated with the emotion, then it can be easier to overlook the sinful anger Jesus describes here. To that end, he moves away from murder to describe instead the consequences of verbal outbursts. That's not to say murder, or any other physical manifestation of anger, is not a sin. The sixth commandment makes clear that it is, and Jesus has already announced that he will not violate or change any of God's laws (Exodus 20:13). But Christ wants his disciples to understand that we can—and do—sin long before reaching that point.

To that end, he gives two examples of ways that people can react in sinful anger without ever actually injuring the other person (at least not physically).

When our words condemn us

The first is often translated as "insults" and is the Aramaic word *raca*. In the literal sense, it means to be empty-headed or stupid. But in the way Jesus uses it here, he's not talking about saying someone made a dumb choice or did something stupid. Rather, it's saying that the person is stupid. It's a statement about their character and worth as an individual.

And the second example is similar to the first. *More*, often translated as fool, was in many ways the worst, most slanderous insult you could use against a person in ancient Israel. It comes from the Greek word for "moron" and meant a person who is so morally deficient, corrupt, and immoral as to be of little to no value whatsoever.

Now, you and I probably don't have to think very long to remember a time in which we've used similar insults to describe someone. And, to be sure, verbal insults typically have fewer practical consequences than walking up to someone and hitting them—though, depending on the context, that sort of escalation is not out of the question. But we must remember that what we say often offers the clearest insights into the state of our hearts.

As Jesus warns the Pharisees later on in Matthew's gospel, "out of the abundance of the heart the mouth speaks" (Matthew 12:34). James echoes those sentiments when he cautions that "if anyone thinks he is religious and does not bridle his tongue but deceives his heart, this person's religion is worthless" (James 1:26). Later on in that same letter, James adds that "the tongue is a fire, a world of unrighteousness. . . . staining the whole body, setting on fire the entire course of life, and set on fire by hell" (James 3:6).

It can be tempting, at times, to let our mouths run when we're angry and say things out of frustration that we would not say otherwise. But we must never underestimate the damage that a careless word can do.

Most of us understand that basic truth, though. We know that it's wrong to insult others and speak of them in a way that tears them down rather than builds them up. Yet, all of us do it from time to time, and the moments in which those words are motivated by anger are often the most damaging. That's why Jesus is so emphatic that we must address the anger we allow to linger in our hearts before it makes its way out into the open, a point he makes clear in the next verses by referencing one of the holiest moments that your average Jewish person in ancient Israel could experience.

When our actions reveal us

"Offering your gift at the altar," as Jesus describes in verse 23, was a special and sacred experience for God's people. Very rarely were non-priests allowed before the altar at the Temple in Jerusalem. Even then, they were allowed only when bringing animal sacrifices for a special occasion. Some would prepare for years, or all of their lives, for this moment.

Yet Jesus says that even in the midst of such a sacred event, if you "remember that your brother has something against you, leave your gift there before the altar and go. First be reconciled to your brother, and then come and offer your gift" (Matthew 5:23–24).

Such an act would have been unthinkable for the crowds listening to Jesus. It would perhaps be akin to leaving the baptistry after wading into the water or stopping halfway down the aisle on the day of your wedding. Such sacrifices were important, special ceremonies at the heart of the Jewish religion. Yet Jesus places a higher priority on being in right relationship with other people. Why?

The most reasonable explanation is that he knows we can't be in a right relationship with God if we're knowingly allowing ourselves to be in a broken relationship with his children.

That point is further reinforced in the following verses, where he describes the urgency with which we should come to terms with our accuser in order to avoid bringing the matter before a judge. In both examples, he calls his disciples to take the initiative in seeking to fix what our anger and sins have broken, with the clear warning that judgment awaits any who fail to do so.

And, though the sin is different, the basic warning is the same in the next statement as well.

Lust

The second of Christ's "You have heard it said" statements deals with the sin of lust. He begins, "You have heard that it was said, 'You shall not commit adultery.' But I say to you that everyone who looks at a woman with lustful intent has already committed adultery with her in his heart" (Matthew 5:27–28).

As with anger, Christ's focus in this passage is not meant to dilute or diminish the sinfulness or consequences of acting on that lust physically. Adultery—like murder—is expressly forbidden in the Ten Commandments and remains a sin with devastating consequences for those who commit it (Exodus 20:14). Rather, he is once again making the point that the sin starts long before it ever reaches the point of action. As such, it is important that we combat the sin at its source rather than attempting to clean up the mess it makes after the fact.

Anyone who has ever been forced to grapple with lust—which, to be clear, is all of us to at least some extent—can testify that it becomes increasingly more difficult to address the longer it persists.

Think back to how David's sin with Bathsheba began: "It happened, late one afternoon, when David arose from his couch and was walking on the roof of the king's house, that he saw from the roof a woman bathing; and the woman was very beautiful" (2 Samuel 11:2). David's sin was not noticing the woman, it was in persisting to look and in dwelling on that beauty long after it was initially noticed. Because David allowed that look to turn into lust, he ended up taking Bathsheba into his room, getting her pregnant, deceiving her husband Uriah, and then having Uriah carry his death sentence back with him to the army David should have been leading.

Lust is dangerous, in large part, because it can seem like an insignificant and natural reaction at first. As such, it can be easy to underestimate the consequences if we allow lustful thoughts to persist unchecked. David did not plan on murdering an innocent man or essentially forcing himself on the beautiful woman he saw from his balcony. Yet, that's exactly what happened because he chose to address the consequences of his sin rather than the sin itself.

What happened to David can happen to any of us—though perhaps to a lesser degree. So Christ commands us to do whatever is necessary to address the sin before it escalates.

Address sins sooner than later

It probably goes without saying that when Jesus advocates for plucking out an eye or cutting off a hand in this passage, he is being a bit hyperbolic. After all, even a blind person can lust, so altering our physical capacities is not a foolproof barrier to sin. Rather, Jesus is once again highlighting the urgency with which we should approach addressing our sins as they arise.

The Greek word used in Matthew 5:29 to describe such sins—*skandalizei*—speaks clearly to why such urgency is required. It comes from the word *skandalethron*, which refers to the stick on which bait was placed in a trap. The stick itself posed a minor threat outside of the trap, but any who took the bait quickly discovered that it was attached to something much more dangerous.

In the same way, sins like lust may seem minor and relatively harmless by themselves. But when we allow them to linger—to take the proverbial bait—it won't take long to realize that they were a gateway to far greater peril. And all of us have something in our lives that the Devil loves to use for that purpose, some pet sin to which we are particularly vulnerable.

Do you know what that sin is for you?

Oftentimes, God is the only one who knows the root cause of the struggles we face. When we try to fix ourselves, we often end up just treating the symptoms and then wondering why nothing seems to be getting better.

Generally, the real reason for our sin differs substantially from the way in which it manifests. With adultery, for example, many couples have come to find that while lust was a cause for a person's infidelity, issues of neglect, insecurity, and a host of other faults contributed just as much, if not more, to the sinful act.

So as you seek to address the sins in your life—be it lust, anger, or any others—be sure to include God in the conversation. Just know that there is little the Lord can do to help if we are not willing to act in obedience to what he tells us.

While that obedience will not extend to the point of self-mutilation, if there is any area of our lives we are unwilling to open up to a bit of spiritual surgery, then our issues with sin are not going to get any better.

Jesus continues to address that temptation to manage our sin rather than eliminate it in the third of his "You have heard it said" statements.

Divorce

The next issue to which Jesus speaks is divorce.

In Christ's culture, divorce was a far more common practice than God ever intended. The Jews typically allowed divorce for any reason. In the Mishna, for example, Beit Hillel said that something as simple as burning or oversalting a dish provided defensible grounds for separation while Rabbi Akiva argued that a man could divorce his wife if he found someone more attractive. In fact, divorce was so common during this time that many women were hesitant to even get married.

To divorce his wife, the husband simply presented her with a certificate of divorce that simply stated "And this that you shall have from me is a scroll of divorce, and a letter of leave, and a bill of dismissal to go to marry any man that you wish."

The relationship that was meant to serve as an example of God's faithfulness to his people had devolved into a transaction so flippant that it served little purpose at all. As such, it is perhaps the clearest example of the relaxing of God's commandments against which Christ warned back in verse 19.

No one who was primarily concerned with honoring the Lord would argue that rampant divorce was a permissible way to avoid the sin of adultery. The only way to reach that conclusion is to have the avoidance of sin rather than the acceptance of God's will as one's primary focus. That the solution from the religious leaders to not breaking the seventh commandment was to undermine the sanctity of marriage rather than address the sin of lust speaks volumes about the state of Judaism during the time of Christ.

But while it would be easy to castigate the scribes and Pharisees, how often do we attempt the same kinds of solutions today?

The truth is that the vast majority of God's commands are clear and easy to understand—especially those that deal with morality. Often, our attempts to contextualize or explain why our versions of the sins Scripture forbids are different than those the Lord condemned are not all that different from the way the Jews came to see marriage.

Eugene Peterson describes this temptation well in his translation of these verses: "Remember the Scripture that says, 'Whoever divorces his wife, let him do it legally, giving her divorce papers and her legal rights'? Too many of you are using that as a cover for selfishness and whim, pretending to be righteous because you are 'legal.' Please, no more pretending. . . . You can't use legal cover to mask a moral failure." (Matthew 5:31–32, MSG).

Conclusion

In many ways, Christ's plea of "Please, no more pretending" sums up his arguments against each of the sins addressed in these first three statements.

As mentioned at the start, one of the primary reasons that anger, lust, and divorce proved to be so dangerous to Jesus' original audience, as well as to us today, is because these sins can seem easy to ignore. We cannot afford to wait to address these moral failings until they have manifested in action, but far too often that's exactly what we try to do.

So before we continue this conversation in the next chapter, take some time to ask God to reveal any areas of your life where you are "pretending."

Then ask him to help you know what measures you need to take in order to address those sins right now so that they do not continue to fester and grow in your heart.

And commit to following through with whatever he calls you to do.

4

Prioritize your witness

Matthew 5:33–48
(oaths, retaliation, love your enemies)

In the last chapter, we looked at what we called the three private "You have heard it said" statements Jesus made in Matthew 5.

We classified them as private in nature, even though they related to how one interacted with others, because they pertained closely to how we choose to respond to the issues of anger and lust, with divorce in many ways an extension of the conversation about lust.

The manifestation of those sins is often kept private because most people tend to understand, at least on some level, that it is wrong to act on them.

Such is not always the case, however, with the issues discussed in this chapter: taking oaths, retaliating when wronged, and hating those who hate us.

While some of the same elements from the first three will apply to these commands as well, the latter three subjects were considered largely defensible actions in both ancient Israel and in our culture today. By looking at each through the lens of its impact on our witness, we can begin to understand why Jesus calls us to a higher standard than was often found in his day and in our own.

Oaths

In Matthew 5:33, when Jesus begins the fourth statement with "Again you have heard that it was said to those of old, 'You shall not swear falsely, but shall perform to the Lord what you have sworn,'" he was not directly quoting any particular text. Rather, it was a summarization of teachings from Leviticus 19, Numbers 30, and Deuteronomy 23. The basic teaching is easy to decipher, though: don't lie.

But what is a lie?

The obvious answer revolves around sharing something you know to be untrue. However, withholding information and issuing half-truths, exaggerations, slander, and misrepresentations should be considered lying as well. Essentially, anything but the whole truth fails to meet God's standard.

The Bible is consistent in its teaching on the importance of truth:

1. "These are the things that you shall do: Speak the truth to one another; render in your gates judgments that are true and make for peace" (Zechariah 8:16). Truth is important in all circumstances and for all people.

2. "Stand therefore, having fastened on the belt of truth" (Ephesians 6:14). Truth is part of God's intended protection against the dangers of sin.

3. "The getting of treasures by a lying tongue is a fleeting vapor and a snare of death" (Proverbs 21:6). The temporary gains from lying never outweigh their eventual consequences.

4. "Lying lips are an abomination to the LORD, but those who act faithfully are his delight" (Proverbs 12:22). The Lord is pleased when we tell the truth, even if others are not.

5. "Do not lie to one another, seeing that you have put off the old self with its practices" (Colossians 3:9). Lying should not characterize the life of someone who has been saved by Jesus. It is a habit of our old selves that was washed away by the mercy and grace of God.

Yet, despite Scripture's repeated warnings against lies, the culture of Christ's day was far more flippant when it came to the truth.

In the first century, most Jews believed that the only oaths that were truly binding were those made on God. If you swore by anything other than the Lord—your head, Jerusalem, or even heaven—then you left yourself a way out of the promise you had made.

While this distinction may seem arbitrary to us, it had become an accepted practice in large part because of the well-intentioned gap that people drew between God and everything else.

The postexilic Jews held God in such high esteem—and rightly so—that nothing else compared to his glory or importance. Rather than elevating the Lord, however, that gap eventually worked to diminish everything else. As a result, anything not considered sacred was deemed of little enough value that one could swear by it without angering God.

The influence of Greek philosophy likely played a role as well. The Greeks taught that there was a strong distinction between the body and soul, which eventually crossed over to sacred and secular divisions in other parts of the culture as well. Carrying this thinking over to today, it would be similar to saying that as long as you didn't lie at church, God wouldn't care if you lied at work or at school or at home.

The problem with this approach, both in the ancient world and today, is that our God is not confined to a certain location. He is equally present everywhere and claims equal ownership over every facet of our lives and the world in which we live. As such, there is no separation between the sacred and the secular because he is Lord over all of it.

That's why Jesus commanded his followers not to "take an oath at all, either by heaven, for it is the throne of God, or by the earth, for it is his footstool, or by Jerusalem, for it is the city of the great King. And do not take an oath by your head, for you cannot make one hair white or black. Let what you say be simply 'Yes' or 'No'; anything more than this comes from evil" (Matthew 5:34–37).

Oaths are only necessary when our character and past actions give people reason to doubt that they can trust us. If we have to rely on the credibility of something outside of ourselves to convince people that we're telling the truth, then we have much larger problems to address.

Christ's purpose in warning against oaths is intended to remind us that we should never take our integrity for granted. Every lie we tell—no matter how seemingly insignificant or unrelated to our faith—diminishes our ability to share the gospel effectively because, ultimately, the credibility of Christ depends on the credibility of Christians.

That emphasis on how our everyday decisions can impact the validity of our witness caries over to the second "You have heard it said" statement.

Retaliation

Christ's message against retaliation begins with "You have heard that it was said, 'An eye for an eye and a tooth for a tooth.' But I say to you, Do not resist the one who is evil" (Matthew 5:38–39). Whereas his previous statement was a summation of several texts, here he quotes directly from Exodus 21:23–24: "But if there is harm, then you shall pay life for life, eye for eye, tooth for tooth, hand for hand, foot for foot, burn for burn, wound for wound, stripe for stripe."

This admonition was not unique to the Jewish faith, however. It appears as far back as the Code of Hammurabi, an ancient Babylonian law that had been around for nearly eighteen hundred years by the time of Jesus.

Yet, it is important to note that the intent of this command was not to enable retribution as much as to restrain it.

It's human nature not to feel vindicated until the other person has suffered as much as we have. For most cultures across history, that idea is at the center of justice. The problem is that we tend to be horrible judges of how much we have actually suffered.

As such, when left to our own devices, we will often inflict greater harm on those who've hurt us than we've endured ourselves. Such actions create a cycle of vengeance that can quickly escalate, with disastrous consequences.

So God mandated a rule among his people—one so common sense as to have been derived by other cultures as well—that took the responsibility for determining a just punishment out of the hands of those who had been hurt in order to provide a path to a more peaceful resolution.

In so doing, he also created a system by which accountability could be dealt out regardless of the wronged individual's capacity to achieve it themselves. Strength, influence, and wealth were no longer prerequisites for justice—at least in theory—and a more stable society was made possible in the effort.

Overall, it sounds like a solid approach.

So why did Jesus want to change it?

To understand Christ's command, it's important to note that at no time does he deny that we have the right to resist or retaliate when wronged.

He just calls us to *choose* not to do so.

The fact that we retain our right to do otherwise is what will make it stand out so much when we choose not to get pulled into the cycle of retaliation.

And to show us what that principle looks like in action, he gives us four examples.

Value your witness

The first regards our honor: "If anyone slaps you on the right cheek, turn to him the other also" (Matthew 5:39).

In Jesus' day, whenever someone would slap another person, they would almost always use their right hand. As such, in order to slap the right cheek, you would have to use the back of your hand. This kind of strike was the height of insult in the ancient world, but it did not indicate a serious threat to one's safety. This distinction reveals two crucial aspects of Christ's instruction in this verse.

The first pertains to what he is *not* telling us. Jesus is not saying that it would be wrong for us to defend ourselves against legitimate danger. If someone attacks with the intent to do real, physical harm, then you are free to defend yourself and others without violating this command. Could there be instances where God would call us to allow ourselves to be injured or killed? Yes, and martyrs throughout Christian history speak to that possibility. But it is not a given for every situation and should be seen as the exception rather than the rule.

The second truth is that we are called to resist the temptation to respond in kind when people insult, demean, or attempt to draw us into the kinds of spats that so often result in both parties looking foolish and immature in the end. Again, we have every right to defend ourselves against such an attack, but Christ calls us to choose not to do so. The risk that we would do more harm to our witness over the course of our response is far greater than the risk associated with letting the insult go unreturned, and our witness must remain a higher priority than our pride.

The same basic principle applies to the second example as well. Jesus continued: "And if anyone would sue you and take your tunic, let him have your cloak as well" (Matthew 5:40).

In Exodus 22, the Law states that someone could sue and take your tunic as collateral against debts to which they were entitled, but they were forbidden from taking your cloak as well (Exodus 22:26–27). For those who were poor, the cloak served not only as an outer garment but also as a blanket or a bed during the night. To take it was to leave a person vulnerable to the elements and, as such, violated the basic rights that the Lord granted his people.

Consequently, a person's cloak, in many ways, came to epitomize the idea of an essential possession in Israel. Yet, Jesus calls us to be willing to give it up, even though we have every right to keep it. Again, the basic point has less to do with a particular article of clothing than demonstrating that the followers of Christ are called to a higher standard than the culture around us. However, it is a standard to which we must choose to adhere, and doing so will require us to accept outcomes that will not always seem fair.

Whereas the second example pertained to our possessions, the third relates to our time.

In Jesus' day, Roman soldiers were permitted to force Jews to carry their packs for up to one mile. It didn't matter if you were headed in the opposite direction, in a hurry, or even had your hands full already. As you might guess, no one outside of the army was a fan of this practice. Many listening on the mountainside that day would have likely endured this inconvenience, perhaps even as they had traveled to hear Jesus speak.

Given that context, you can imagine what the people's reaction would have been when Jesus told them that instead of carrying the pack for only the first mile, they should carry it for two (Matthew 5:41). And most of us would probably feel the same today. Surrendering our time to the Lord is among the most difficult sacrifices he asks of us, but it can also be the key to earning the opportunity to share the gospel with others. Many of Christ's most impactful interactions began because he took the time to make people feel valued, and the same can be true for us when we surrender our time to the Lord.

In the final example, Jesus commands us to "give to the one who begs from you, and do not refuse the one who would borrow from you" (Matthew 5:42). It is important to note, however, that he is not calling us to be foolish with our resources or to give to the point that we can no longer provide for our family. After all, the Bible is very clear on the importance of being good stewards of that which God has given us, and the biblical commands regarding sharing money are aimed largely at achieving fairness among the Lord's people (2 Corinthians 8:13-14).

Still, it can be easy to claim stewardship as a guise for greed.

Far too often, we neglect to use the resources God has given us to help those in need without ever asking him if we are right to do so. And Jesus is clear that when we pray, our focus should be "Lord, how can I help them?" rather than "Lord, do I have to help them?". Applying that perspective to our resources enables us to demonstrate the love of God and adhere to his priorities in ways that go beyond the basic requirements of being a good person.

Over the course of five short verses, Jesus commands us to value our witness above our reputation, possessions, time, and resources. He makes the point with each that the basics of the Law and the expectations of others do not require us to do so and that adhering to his standards is a choice we must make because it will never be required of us.

Still, it is a choice that can have a profound impact on our ability to share the gospel effectively and demonstrates the difference that a relationship with him should make in the day-to-day aspects of our lives.

And he makes that distinction even more plainly in the final of his "You have heard it said" statements.

Love your enemies

The last illustration Jesus uses in this section is perhaps the most well-known. It begins "You have heard that it was said, 'You shall love your neighbor and hate your enemy.' But I say to you, Love your enemies and pray for those who persecute you, so that you may be sons of your Father who is in heaven" (Matthew 5:43–45).

Most of us are probably familiar with the first part of that statement. The command to "love your neighbor" is one of the pillars of Judeo-Christian morality. The Jews were told in Leviticus 19:18 to "love your neighbor as yourself," and Jesus would reiterate this instruction when challenged by the religious leaders, placing it second in importance only to the command to "love the Lord your God with all your heart and with all your soul and with all your mind" (Matthew 22:37–40).

The second part, however, might seem more foreign to us.

After all, nowhere in Scripture does God command us to hate our enemies, yet Jesus includes that in his statement as if it would have been considered conventional wisdom to those listening. Unfortunately, it was.

The rabbis of Jesus' day considered all of their fellow Jews to be their neighbors and everyone else—the Gentiles—to be their spiritual enemies. The rabbis were afraid that the Gentile world would corrupt God's people, so they instructed their fellow Jews to avoid all association with outsiders to the point that they were considered a vile threat.

However, this solution to dealing with the sinful world around us has not been historically confined to those in ancient Israel. Even today, we do not have to look hard to find Christian communities so insulated that they have little interaction with the world around them. And the rhetoric painting the culture as our enemies rather than our mission field has only grown stronger in recent years. Why, then, should we be surprised when the lost around us reciprocate the feeling and treat us as their enemies as well?

As Jesus makes clear in the subsequent verses, even the most sinful in our society are capable of loving those who love them. Christ calls us to something greater, and he tells us that the best place to start is by praying for those our natural inclinations would lead us to hate.

Be sure that when you pray, however, your prayers are for the well-being and blessing of the other person. We are not praying in love if we're essentially asking God to smite those we dislike or who have been mean to us. It can be tempting, though, to let the bulk of our prayers consist of trying to make the Lord aware of their sins when he knows them even better than we do and yet loves them still.

When that is our approach, our hearts are not aligned with his and cannot be transformed in a way that will result in the kind of love to which we are called.

Yet, when we pray as our Lord did, asking the Father to forgive those who have wronged us and seeking to be a blessing to them even when they have been nothing but a curse to us, we live out our calling as the children of God.

Conclusion

Eugene Peterson described the approach outlined in this chapter well in his translation of the final verse in this passage: "In a word, what I'm saying is, *Grow up*. You're kingdom subjects. Now live like it. Live out your God-created identity. Live generously and graciously toward others, the way God lives toward you" (Matthew 5:48, MSG).

That is the kind of perfection to which Christ calls us. God knows that we will make mistakes, but we must never allow the inevitability of our failings to become excuses for doing so.

The Greek word most often translated as perfect in verse 48 is *teleioi*, and it does not mean that something exists without flaws but rather that it is well suited to the purpose for which it was created. God created us to love him and, through that love, care for others in the same way he does.

That is the heart of the gospel message, and we are perfect as our Father is perfect to the extent that we extend his love and message of salvation to others, regardless of whether we would consider them to be friends, enemies, or something in between.

Such a purpose requires, however, that we prioritize our witness and mission above our own ease, our own rights, and our own definitions of love. Essentially, we are to love God more than ourselves and allow him to define the standards to which we are held.

But, as we'll see in the next chapter, God's standards pertain to more than just our actions. So with that in mind, let's continue by looking at what Jesus says about giving to the needy, prayer, fasting, and storing up treasures in heaven.

5

Serve secretly

Matthew 6:1–24

(giving, prayer, fasting, treasures)

So far in the Sermon on the Mount, Jesus has described the character required to experience God's blessings. He's also called his disciples to live out their faith in a way that brings glory to God and draws people into a relationship with their heavenly Father. He then established that a correct understanding of the law and the prophets should call people to a sense of righteousness that surpasses the self-reliant morality of the religious leaders.

Next, he gave a series of six statements demonstrating how such righteousness applies to more than the avoidance of overt sins. Doing the right thing is important, but the motivation behind our actions is just as relevant as the actions themselves. To that end, he continues the discussion in Matthew 6 by demonstrating how "acts of righteousness" will not result in righteousness unless they are done for God's glory rather than our own.

But how can we gauge the degree to which our motivations are truly in accordance with God's will?

And even if we are motivated more by building up treasures in heaven rather than receiving the praise of people, is that enough to align our hearts with the Lord's? Or is there still a degree of sinful selfishness in the pursuit of such treasures that we must overcome?

Those are difficult questions, and the answers will vary for each of us. Fortunately, Jesus gives us some guidelines by which we can evaluate our own motives and better judge whose glory we are really pursuing.

When attention becomes problematic

In Matthew 6:1, Jesus declares, "Beware of practicing your righteousness before other people in order to be seen by them, for then you will have no reward from your Father who is in heaven." The phrase "seen by them" is the Greek word *theathenai*, and it's where we get the word *theater*. It literally means "for the purpose of being seen by others."

The component of intent to that phrase is crucial for understanding Christ's teachings in the verses that follow.

It is not wrong to be seen when following God's will or serving him. After all, Jesus was quite clear in Matthew 5 that a key component of being his disciple means being a light for the world and a city on a hill. Jesus would be a hypocrite if he followed that instruction by commanding that we then shun all attention. Instead, both in Matthew 5:16 and in these passages in chapter 6, Jesus makes clear that such attention only becomes an issue when it becomes our focus.

To illustrate that point in practice, he gives three examples of commonplace aspects of religious life—at least, they were commonplace in his time—that could easily be done for the wrong reasons. He then concludes the argument by discussing treasures in heaven and the need to choose where our greatest allegiance will reside.

Giving to the needy

The first of those examples pertains to giving.

In Matthew 6:2, Jesus instructs his disciples, "Thus, when you give to the needy, sound no trumpet before you, as the hypocrites do in the synagogues and in the streets, that they may be praised by others."

Notice that Jesus says *when* you give to the needy. In Jewish society, giving alms was mandatory. It had been a requirement of the Lord since their ancestors wandered in the wilderness (Deuteronomy 15:7–8, 10–11). So Jesus' concern was not whether the people would help the poor, but whether they would do so for God's glory or for theirs.

And, to be sure, quite a bit of glory could be gained in Jewish society for those who gave extravagantly.

The most common means of giving in the first century were the *Tamhui*, or daily collection, and the *Kuppah*, a collection taken every Friday. These offerings were usually given at the synagogue, at the Temple, or in another public location.

Consequently, giving these alms in secret was not really possible. However, because the area was so often populated, you were also not likely to stand out unless you made a show of your giving.

Such a show is what Jesus referred to when he mentioned sounding trumpets in association with one's giving.

A good bit of speculation has occurred over the years as to what exactly Jesus was referring to with this phrase.

Some have speculated that there was a horn-shaped opening in boxes used for receiving people's offerings. Since people paid in coins, you can imagine how easy it would be to make a good deal of noise with a sizeable donation if that were the case.

Others have argued that the trumpets refer to the horns that would sound when announcing the start of the fast or calling people to some religious observation. That's when the most people would be paying attention so, if you waited to give until that moment, your offering would garner the greatest visibility.

The most likely explanation, though, is that the phrase was simply an idiom commonly understood to mean something along the lines of "toot your own horn" today.

Ultimately, the basic meaning seems clear, and Jesus was equally clear in condemning the "hypocrites" who engaged in such practices.

By contrast, he called his disciples not to "let your left hand know what your right hand is doing" because "your Father who sees in secret will reward you" (Matthew 6:3–4).

However, the nature of that reward can also prove to be an impediment to keeping God's glory as our first priority.

How do I give for God's glory (and not my own)?

More will be said about storing up treasures in heaven later in this chapter, but it's important to note that God's rewards are not restricted to the next life.

Our heavenly Father desires to bless us in this life as well. That's why Jesus began the Sermon by going into the kind of character that positions us to receive those blessings. As we discussed in the opening chapter, though, the nature of those blessings is often quite different from the kind of prosperity-gospel yearnings that have led many otherwise well-meaning Christians astray.

Our giving does not ensure we will be economically blessed or that we will escape hardship. When we give in order to receive personal gains such as these, we are making the same fundamental mistake as when we give for the adulation of others; namely, our motivations are still self-centered.

This misconception was especially prevalent in Jesus' day, as wealth and status were seen as clear signs of God's blessings, while poverty and all that accompanied it were seen as a sign of his disfavor.

Jesus spends much of his ministry trying to help people move away from this transactional type of relationship with the Lord, and parables like the Rich Man and Lazarus demonstrate clearly that we err greatly when we mistake material abundance for God's blessing (Luke 16:19–31).

Ultimately, God's rewards—in whatever form they take—exist to draw us into closer communion with him because there is no greater blessing we could attain than a thriving relationship with our heavenly Father. When we give for his glory rather than our own, we demonstrate that our hearts are well positioned to receive the rewards he has in mind. When the reverse is true, rewarding our giving would simply reinforce the kind of behavior that drives us further from him.

So what does giving for God's glory look like on a practical level?

Jesus certainly wasn't saying that it's wrong to put money in the offering on Sunday because someone might see you do it. Again, not all public giving is bad.

After all, in the early church it was common for people who owned land or a house to sell them and put the money "at the apostles' feet" (Acts 4:32–35). This sort of giving was not condemned because it was done for the right reasons, and the same is true for us today.

So rather than embrace a legalistic approach to giving, get into the habit of asking God how he wants you to give.

It could be that he wants to use your gift as an example to others and as an opportunity to glorify his name. Or it could be that he wants you to give in secret.

Whatever the case may be, trust that God knows your heart better than even you do, and whatever his answer is will be what is best for your relationship with him.

With the necessity of such prayer in mind, let's turn now to Christ's next example.

Prayer

Jesus begins his second application on the principle of acting for God's glory rather than our own by stating, "And when you pray, you must not be like the hypocrites. For they love to stand and pray in the synagogues and at the street corners, that they may be seen by others. Truly, I say to you, they have received their reward" (Matthew 6:5).

Again, Jesus assumes that anyone who would claim to be his disciple is already committed to prayer. He does not feel the same need to justify why people should pray, as is often the case today. (See Dr. Jim Denison's book *The Greater Work* for practical insights on the necessity and function of prayer.) Jesus understood that those in attendance were in the habit of praying, and the assurance that they would continue to do so only increased the urgency of making sure it was done with the proper motivation.

It is often the most consistent and fundamental parts of our walk with the Lord that can pose the greatest threat to our spiritual health. For first-century Jews, giving and fasting would have been of equal importance to prayer in this regard. For us today, that is often not the case. While we can discuss the degree to which that needs to change some other time, that reality makes prayer perhaps the most relevant and relatable of the three examples Jesus gives in this passage. If we can learn to recognize Satan's temptations when it comes to prayer, then we will be better equipped to recognize those same strategies when applied to other areas of our walk with the Lord.

Satan is smart, and he knows that if he can corrupt something as foundational as prayer then the rest of our walk with God will begin to falter as well. And one of the most effective ways that he can attack prayer is by shifting its focus from the Lord to us. Unfortunately, that's exactly what he had done with the "hypocrites" to whom Jesus refers in each of the three applications found in this passage.

Who were the hypocrites?

Hypocrite comes from the Greek word *hypokritai*. In the ancient world, it referred to actors who wore different masks to portray various characters on the stage. In the context of this verse, the hypocrites were those who performed religious acts for the attention and admiration of other people rather than as an act of worship to the Lord. And the larger context of the Sermon leaves little doubt as to who these religious performers were in the first century.

The reference to the righteousness of the scribes and Pharisees in Matthew 5:20, coupled with the six statements comparing their teachings with the truth of God's word in the rest of the chapter, point clearly to the religious leaders as the hypocrites to whom Jesus refers in chapter 6.

Later on in his ministry, Jesus would make that connection even clearer when he told a parable about a Pharisee who did exactly what Christ warned against in these verses (Luke 18:9–14). Both then and in Matthew 6, the basic teaching is the same: those who pray in order to garner the attention of others will be ignored by God.

Ironically, their desire to be seen as righteous and pious by the crowds ultimately demonstrates how deficient they actually are in those qualities. Even if others may not be able to discern the difference, God can, and he does not take kindly to people using worship as a platform for self-adulation.

By contrast, the true purpose of prayer is to bring us into communion with the Lord. Relying on the "empty phrases" and "many words" that Jesus criticizes in verse 7 reveals a severe misunderstanding of the Father's character and what kind of relationship he wants to have with his people. In short, praying in this manner treats the true God like one of the heathen gods that had to be convinced through repetition to act on behalf of their supporters. The scene in 1 Kings 18 where Elijah faces off with the prophets of Baal illustrates this point well (1 Kings 18:20–40). What was true of the Lord then is still true of the Lord today, and our prayers should reflect that reality.

So, with that principle in mind, Jesus turns to instructing his disciples on the proper way to pray.

How then should we pray?

While we do not have the space to go in depth into the example Jesus gives in Matthew 6:9–13, the Lord's Prayer is one of the most well-known and commonly cited passages in all of Scripture, and an abundance of teachings exist that go through it verse by verse. Within the larger context of the Sermon on the Mount, however, two key principles stand out.

To begin, the words of this prayer are meant to offer a foundation and guidelines for how to pray to the Lord. This prayer is not a magic formula that must be—or should be—repeated by rote. Rather, it is intended to highlight the basic principles of how we should engage in communication with the Lord. It would be hard to have a deep and meaningful relationship with a friend or with your spouse if you simply said the same things every day. So why would we do that with God?

Even if it's not the words of the Lord's prayer, learning to talk with the Lord as if we were talking to a real person is an invaluable part of engaging with God. At the same time, conversing with the Lord of the Universe should not be taken as lightly as a flippant conversation with a friend.

To that end, Christ's prayer paradigm starts with a recognition of God's holiness and the prioritization of his will above our own. It is only after those two principles are established that our hearts and minds will be in the right place to begin asking for the things we need and desire—"our daily bread," as Jesus puts it.

Even when the focus of our prayer turns to ourselves, though, Christ is clear that we should not lose sight of the fact that chief among those needs is help with our own fallenness.

By bookending our own desires with a recognition of God's greatness on one side and our sinfulness and susceptibility to temptation on the other, we are better protected against the temptation to use prayer as a means of glorifying ourselves.

Jesus continues his discussion of that temptation by speaking next to the issue of fasting.

Fasting

Fasting is perhaps the most extreme of the three examples regarding the use of spiritual means to acquire personal acclaim. Whereas with giving and prayer, there could be some question as to whether a person was performing religious actions for selfish reasons, Jesus is clear that fasting like the hypocrites requires real work and a level of intentionality that goes beyond the other two.

As he describes in Matthew 6:16, the hypocrites "look gloomy" and "disfigure their faces that their fasting may be seen by others." The Pharisees commonly put ash and dirt on their faces when fasting, while some would even go so far as to wear makeup in order to make themselves look more haggardly. They also made it a point to fast on the second and fifth days of the week, claiming that they did so because those were the days Moses made his trips to receive the Law from God on Mt. Sinai (Luke 18:12). However, those also happened to be the days when the Jewish market was usually busiest, and they would be seen by the most people.

Christ's reply was essentially to just go about your day as you normally would. Whether you were fasting or eating, the only people that should know are you and the Lord. If others find out because they see you skip a meal or because you are part of a group that has pledged to fast for a specific purpose, then that's different. But, as with the other examples, we must choose from whom we want to receive our reward, a fact Jesus spells out even more clearly when he discusses treasures in heaven in the next passage.

Treasures in heaven

The final passage we will look at in this chapter pertains to Christ's admonition not to "lay up for yourselves treasures on earth, where moth and rust destroy and where thieves break in and steal, but lay up for yourselves treasures in heaven, where neither moth nor rust destroys and where thieves do not break in and steal" (Matthew 6:19–20).

In these verses, Jesus addresses three of the primary forms of wealth people possessed in his day.

The first, garments, were viewed more as an investment than an article of clothing. Most people in the first century did not swap out their clothes as fashions changed. The only time they would get rid of something is when it was no longer useful, such as when moths would eat holes in them.

The second type of wealth addressed is grain. While most translations render the Greek word *brosis* as "rust," it more literally refers to a creature that eats away at something, like mice or rats. Protecting one's stores of food from pests was a problem with potential life-or-death implications in the ancient world, and one with which Jesus' audience would have been well acquainted.

The third type of wealth is simply money or other possessions. In the first century, many people protected their wealth by burying it in their houses. We see this idea in the Parable of the Talents, where the third servant takes his master's money and puts it in the ground to protect it (Matthew 25:18). However, the walls surrounding a person's home in this day were typically made of mud bricks and adobe, meaning that it was not hard for someone to "break in and steal."

Christ's point with all three examples is clear: there is no such thing as earthly treasure that is truly safe and secure. Even if our wealth survives all the threats it faces in this life, one day death will come to separate us from it. The only investments of our time and resources that are truly secure are the investments made in God's kingdom.

And while those treasures can be difficult for us to fully comprehend, it's important to note that we don't have to wait for eternity to begin reaping the rewards. The actions that lead to heavenly wealth draw us closer to the

Lord in the present as well. The blessings that come from that relationship are like the interest we draw from an investment we allow to continue building. And while we should never expect that interest to manifest in material gains—though there are times when God can choose to bless us in that fashion—we can trust that it will be more than worth whatever it costs to attain.

Moreover, it will also help to ensure that our top priority remains serving God and his kingdom. As Jesus points out, it's human nature for our hearts to follow our treasure, and the result of where our focus resides has implications for every facet of our lives (Matthew 6:21–23).

Conclusion

Ultimately, the point Jesus makes throughout the passages we have examined in this chapter is that we must choose whether our material possessions will serve God or whether we will try to use God to serve ourselves. (*Mamona*, often translated as "money," originally referred to all material possessions.) It is a binary choice, and one that each of us must actively make every day.

The temptation is always going to be to try to manage both, thinking that as long as God remains our top priority, it doesn't matter how small the gap gets between him and whatever comes in second. Unfortunately, that sort of thinking invariably leads to other concerns overtaking the Lord as our focus at some point.

If the gap between God and money, for example, gets small, then when finances get tight, it can be easy for the Lord to fall into second place. In the same way, if we are placed in a position of spiritual leadership—whether in our church, home, or any other context—the attention and pressures of that position can change the way we give, pray, and live out our faith on a daily basis.

Even at the best of times, such concerns will always make it difficult to serve God with pure intent. And he knows that, which is why Jesus warns us to be mindful of our motivations and the temptation to chase earthly rewards at the expense of those our heavenly Father longs to give.

Chief among those rewards is often the ability to experience the kind of peace that comes from knowing we can serve God without thinking about ourselves because we can trust him to take care of us.

It is to understanding that truth and its implications that we turn next.

6

Worry not

Matthew 6:25–7:11

(anxiety; judging; sacred pearls; ask, seek, knock)

In the last chapter, we discussed the need to prioritize God's glory over our own, especially when it comes to acts of worship, as that is the path to rewards in heaven that bear interest on earth by drawing us into a closer relationship with the Lord. Jesus continues that conversation in the passages we will look at for this chapter.

He begins, "Therefore I tell you, do not be anxious about your life, what you will eat or what you will drink, nor about your body, what you will put on. Is not life more than food, and the body more than clothing?" (Matthew 6:25).

The Greek phrase translated here as "do not be anxious" is *me merimnate*, and it carries the idea of being "divided into parts" or "drawn in opposite directions."

We cannot remain focused on what God is doing in the present if our attention is constantly pulled to the future. As he says in verse 34, "Do not be anxious about tomorrow, for tomorrow will be anxious for itself. Sufficient for the day is its own trouble." Corrie Ten Boom echoed that sentiment when she noted that "worry does not empty tomorrow of its sorrow, it empties today of its strength."

And though concerns over what is to come are not the sole source of anxiety in our lives, they are emblematic of the worrying Jesus describes in this passage.

The idea here is not that we never experience the emotion of fear or anxiety. As we discussed with anger and lust in chapter 3, God never commands us how to feel. Rather, his instruction pertains to what we do with those emotions and the degree to which we allow them to control our thoughts and actions.

The sin against which we are warned is feeding our anxiety by dwelling on it instead of giving it back to God and trusting that he not only knows our needs but has a plan to meet them as well. Such faith in the face of fear is important for two primary reasons.

The means for our needs

To start, when we allow our anxieties to fester and grow, then they can quickly become a distraction that removes our focus from the Lord. The "therefore" at the start of verse 25 clearly connects this instruction to Christ's command that we must choose whether we will serve God or ourselves, as we discussed in the previous chapter.

Jesus knows that it's easier for us to trust the Lord when our need for him is not as apparent. Consequently, it's the times when money is tight, or we don't have a clear path to meeting our own needs, that we will be most tempted to shuffle God down our list of priorities. Yet it is precisely then that keeping our focus on the Lord and trusting in his will is most important.

It is worth noting, however, that faith in such instances is not the same as ignorance or naiveté. After all, the sincerity and genuineness for which Jesus advocates throughout this Sermon shows that God isn't looking for a "fake it till you make it" kind of faith. Rather, it's about trusting that our heavenly Father is just as aware and concerned about our very real needs as we are.

To illustrate that point, Jesus asks the crowds to look at the birds in the air and the flowers that dotted the fields around them.

Both the birds and the flowers are cared and provided for by the Lord. Notice, though, that the key to that provision is found in the degree to which they act according to their God-given nature. A bird that sits back and waits for a worm to jump in its mouth will starve, and a flower that does not stretch toward the sun will wither and fade. In the same way, the Lord's provision for our lives is tied directly to our obedience to his will.

God's plan for our lives will include the means to provide for our basic needs. If he is our master and his will is our guide, then our needs will be met in the process. As Jesus says in verse 33, "Seek first the kingdom of God and his righteousness, and all these things will be added to you."

Now, that doesn't mean we will always love the way that he goes about meeting those needs. Christian history is filled with plenty of examples of people who suffered for following his will, and Jesus himself promised that such hardships awaited those who would become his disciples (John 16:33). But God's word also points to the reality that part of his provision is also meant to be found in the larger community of faith.

If we are truly acting as the body of Christ, then there should never be a fellow Christian whose needs go unmet, whether they are in our neighborhood, our city, or even on the other side of the world. The church is plenty big enough to make sure that happens. One of the main reasons that, far too often, we fail to do so is because we are more worried about providing for ourselves than allowing God's will to let us know how to help provide for others.

The witness of our trust

The second reason we must control our fears and give our anxiety back to God is the impact that doing so can have on our witness to others.

Anxiety is common to all people, and dealing with such fear is a struggle to which all of us can relate, even if the specific cause of concern varies from person to person. To illustrate that point, Jesus compares the response he is looking for from his disciples with that of the pagans (Matthew 6:32).

Pagan religions were often characterized by the fears of what their gods would do. That's why they tried so hard to appease them with sacrifices. Their gods were essentially humans with superpowers, and they were just as unreliable and unpredictable as one might expect from a being free to act without constraint. Consequently, they could only be relied upon to care for the needs of people to the extent that those people pleased them, and even then there were no guarantees.

For the pagans, worry was warranted because they had no dependable avenue for help beyond themselves.

With our God, it's the exact opposite.

We don't need to worry because he is constant in taking care of those who love him, and his concern for us is not dependent on our most recent offering. However, when we worry and are anxious about the things he has promised to provide, we are, in essence, treating him like he is no different from the pagan gods he deplores. Such an approach reveals a deficiency in our understanding of his character and nature that will not go unnoticed by the lost around us.

However, it will also not go unnoticed when people see us face these moments of anxiety and come through the other side with a faith that is stronger.

Again, that doesn't mean we never experience the emotions of fear and anxiety or that, when we do, we should hide them. But, for better or worse, the implications of how we choose to respond will reverberate far beyond the present moment.

Yet, such faith is not necessary only when it comes to meeting our physical needs. In fact, it is often in our relationships with others that trusting God to handle the things our natural impulses would lead us to control can be most important.

With that in mind, Jesus continues this discussion by turning to the temptation to be "drawn in opposite directions" by the need to confront sin in ourselves and in those around us.

Do not judge

The first five verses of Matthew 7 are often treated more as a stand-alone passage than viewed within the larger context of the Sermon on the Mount. Those who view them as such are not necessarily wrong to do so. There is a clear warning against holding others to higher standards than we hold ourselves that is both important and relevant on its own. However, that teaching takes on an added depth when viewed in light of the passages around it.

The prohibition against judgment that resides at the heart of these verses is absolute. The nature of that forbidden judgment, however, is more nuanced than it's often treated by those who use this passage to advocate against accountability. The Greek word used here for judgment is *krino*, and it essentially means to subject someone to harsh, sharp, unjust criticism in a habitual way. From this definition, we learn two important things about what Jesus is warning against.

First, Christ is not saying that if you see someone sinning you should allow them to continue without saying something. Jesus will outline the proper way to go about addressing such sins in verse 3, but the general principle is that sin must be addressed, just in a way that does not lead us to sin in the process. That doesn't mean we have to be perfect before we can address the sins of others, but we can't be ignorant of our own shortcomings or else we act as a hypocrite and are likely to do more harm than good.

The second truth we learn from this understanding of judgment is that the proper way to address the sins of others is to do so with the same love and mercy God has used with us. Such an approach does not mean mitigating the gravity or seriousness of a person's mistakes, but it does mean allowing God to guide our efforts at accountability to help make sure that we are not overly critical. Ultimately, our job when holding people accountable is to point them back to the Lord and encourage them to seek his forgiveness. The moment we begin to act as the judge, though, we cross that line.

Judgments deal with more than just our assessment of another person's actions. They extend to the way we respond to that assessment, and, if we refuse to show grace to others, we shouldn't expect them to show grace to us. A key to extending that grace is recognizing how much we need it ourselves.

To that end, Jesus gives the well-known example of attempting to take out a speck of dust in your brother's eye while leaving a log in our own eye. But why are we so tempted to point out those specks when we see them?

Perhaps part of the answer is that God has called each of us to help people know him better. When their actions drive them further from the Lord, we are right to address it so long as we can do so in a way that does not cause us to sin as well. After all, Jesus does say that once we have removed the log from our own eye we should help our brother with the speck in his (Matthew 7:5).

Far too often, though, that more righteous motivation comes as a distant second to the fact that trying to fix other people's faults can be a great way to feel good about ourselves without having to address our own. That hypocritical motivation behind an otherwise righteous act ties directly back to what we discussed in the previous chapter.

If, however, we can keep our focus on the Lord and trust that when it comes to addressing sins—both in ourselves and in others—that his plans are better than our own, then we can let go of the worry and self-righteous indignation that so often leads us to judge others more harshly than is warranted.

William Barclay once wrote, "The fact is that if we realized what some people have to go through, so far from condemning them, we would be amazed that they have succeeded in being as good as they are."

God's ultimate purpose behind judging sin is to bring people into a closer relationship with him, and he is the only one who knows how to do that consistently well. And that need to trust his guidance is equally important for the next verse in the Sermon as well.

Do not throw away what is sacred

One of the more challenging verses in all of the Gospels is Matthew 7:6: "Do not give dogs what is holy, and do not throw your pearls before pigs, lest they trample them underfoot and turn to attack you."

Part of the difficulty with this verse is understanding how it fits into the larger movement of the Sermon on the Mount. Like the preceding five verses, it is often dealt with as a stand-alone statement. It doesn't align neatly as a conclusion to Christ's words on judgment or as an introduction to the teachings that follow.

That said, the lack of a clean fit does not mean its placement was random. The same Holy Spirit who inspired the writing of all Scripture deemed this location to be the best place for this teaching.

So why might that be the case? What insights can we glean from the larger context to help us understand Christ's words?

To start, one of the main reasons people often struggle to know what to do with this verse is that its basic teaching feels overly harsh and out of place in the mouth of Jesus. In first-century Judaism, "dogs" often referred to the *ethnically* impure—namely Gentiles—while "pigs" referred to those deemed *ethically* impure. Given that Jesus did not shy away from ministering to Samaritans and Gentiles (John 4; Luke 7:1–10) while routinely meeting with "tax collectors and sinners" (Matthew 9:10), it seems clear that he could not have been saying that such people did not deserve our time or attention. So what did he mean?

To start, the New Testament makes clear that Jesus came to bring salvation to the entire world but that it had to come to the Jews first (Romans 1:16). At this point in his ministry, he was simply not ready to expand its scope to include the Gentiles openly. Still, he made a point of meeting with those the religious leaders would have considered "pigs" from the start, so that can't be the only purpose of his statement.

It's at this point that the verse's place in the larger context of the Sermon bears fruit.

When a gift is unwelcome

While the part of the verse about dogs and pigs often gets the most attention, Jesus gives his reasoning in the second half. We are not to withhold what is sacred and valuable because the proverbial dogs and pigs are unworthy of receiving them, but rather because those gifts would be unwelcome and unappreciated.

In the context of evangelism, for example, this principle reminds us that if someone has shown that they are completely disinterested in the gospel, then continuing to press them about it is unlikely to prove productive.

That doesn't mean we should give up on them, but we can get to the place where continuing to hit people over the head with God's word does far more harm than good to their long-term prospects of accepting Jesus. And when people reach that point, rather than sit there and continue listening to you tell them how much they need the Lord, they may choose to trample you—and the message—simply to get away.

It is important to rely on the Holy Spirit's discernment to know when people reach that point and just need some space. However, giving them that space does not in any way preclude you from living the gospel around them. Oftentimes, seeing Christ's impact on your life can do more to break down any barriers that might exist than your words ever could.

Ultimately, God knows their heart and their mind better than we can. He understands when the sacred pearls of the gospel will be welcome and when they are likely to be discarded. And while his word promises that it will never return void, that is only when it is sent out according to his will (Isaiah 55:11).

If we want to see the lost come to know Jesus, then we must trust that God's plans and his timing are better than our own.

That admonition is key to understanding the final passage we will examine in this chapter.

Ask, seek, knock

Throughout the Sermon, Jesus repeats the theme of needing not to be "drawn in opposite directions" when it comes to trusting in God's guidance over our own. But he transitions toward a different focus beginning in Matthew 7:12. As such, verses 7–11 form a fitting conclusion to the present discussion.

They begin with a series of commands: "Ask and it will be given to you; seek, and you will find; knock, and it will be opened to you" (Matthew 7:7). Those commands are followed with a series of promises: "Everyone who asks receives, and the one who seeks finds, and to the one who knocks it will be opened" (7:8).

But has that been your experience?

I can think of many times when it feels like I asked and was ignored, that I sought God and found nothing, and that I knocked on a door that appeared to remain shut. Chances are, you can as well.

So how do we reconcile that experience with the promises of Jesus?

Some would argue that when the Lord does not appear to answer, it's because we did not ask with sufficient faith. However, Jesus tells his disciples that they can move mountains with faith the size of a mustard seed and honors a father's request to "help my unbelief" (Matthew 17:20; Mark 9:24).

Is some measure of faith necessary to relate properly to the Lord? Absolutely. But does he refuse to bless us because we fail to meet some arbitrary and unknown standard of belief? That idea is both unbiblical and contrary to the heavenly Father Jesus describes in this passage.

As he says in the very next verses, "Which one of you, if his son asks him for bread, will give him a stone? Or if he asks for a fish, will give him a serpent? If you then, who are evil, know how to give good gifts to your children, how much more will your Father who is in heaven give good things to those who ask him!" (Matthew 7:9–11).

Bread in ancient Israel often bore a close resemblance to the sun-parched stones one would encounter on the roads that traversed the county. In fact, many of those in attendance had likely passed by such stones on their way to hear Jesus. Likewise, snakes were commonly found among the fish and eels caught in the lakes of first-century Judea but were considered unclean to eat.

In both examples, the idea is that no good father would trick their child into trying to eat something that was bad for them. The pagan gods that Jesus warned us not to confuse with the one, true God might have done such a thing, but our heavenly Father would not. But, again, has that always been your experience with God? If not, why not?

The answer often goes back to the larger theme we've been discussing in this chapter.

What we ask for vs. what we need

By this point in the Sermon, Jesus has established that God is both aware of our needs and more than capable of meeting them. However, he has also made clear that he will only meet our needs when we trust him enough to accept his provision, even when it may not be what we were hoping to receive.

To a hungry child riding on the roads or sitting by the sea in ancient Israel, it's easy to imagine a rock or snake looking tasty to their naïve eyes. It's also easy to imagine such a child becoming incensed when their father refuses to give them what they are so certain they want.

When we allow our anxieties and worries to make us doubt the faithfulness of our heavenly Father, it can be easy to become that petulant child. We feel the rumble in our stomachs, see what appears to be an appetizing answer, and cannot understand why God would refuse to grant our request.

But if we look back again at the end of verse 11, Jesus does not promise that our heavenly Father will give us the gifts for which we ask. Rather, he promises to give us *good* gifts when we ask.

This side of heaven, we may not always understand how God's answers to our prayers could be considered good. However, he has given us more than enough evidence to trust that they are.

Such trust in our heavenly Father's direction for our lives is the only way to combat the anxiety and need for control that can make it so difficult to follow his will. But, as he describes in the remainder of the Sermon on the Mount, it's also the only way to experience the blessings of a personal relationship with him.

7

Build on the rock

Matthew 7:12–27
(Golden rule, narrow gates, fruit trees, and solid foundations)

"So whatever you wish that others would do to you, do also to them, for this is the Law and the Prophets" (Matthew 7:12).

Thus begins the final new teaching of the Sermon on the Mount. The rest of Matthew 7 revolves largely around Christ's encouragement to put his words into practice, but the "Golden Rule"—as it's been known since John Wesley first called it that in 1750—serves as the summation of all that has come before it. Jesus' teachings on the nature of blessings, righteousness, sin, individual rights, service to him, and worry all find their fulfillment in this single thought. If we can get this right, then all of the Law and the Prophets will fall into place.

Take the social parts of the Ten Commandments, for example. Do you want others to murder or harm you? To commit adultery with your spouse? To steal from you? To lie to or about you? To gossip and slander about you? To covet what's yours? If the world practiced the Golden Rule, then we wouldn't have to worry about any of that.

What would be the consequences for our prisons and jails if there were no more murder, physical assault, or theft? For our families if there were no more adultery? For our relationships if there were no more lies, slander, gossip, or coveting?

Life as we know it would be utterly transformed. Sadly, people tend not to live by the Golden Rule, including most Christians. We may wish it's how others would behave, but we seldom do so ourselves.

More often, people aspire to a lesser standard, and that was the case in the first century as well.

A similar thought to the Golden Rule was present in the ethics and philosophy of other thinkers around this time, with Rabbi Hillel's coming closest to the standards of Jesus: "What is hateful to you, do not do to your neighbor; that is the entire Torah; the rest is commentary." However, Jesus was the first to phrase it positively, and the difference is substantial.

If you see a car broken down on the side of the road, Hillel would tell you not to hinder or harm the person while Jesus tells you to stop and help. If you notice a lonely colleague at work or student at school, Hillel says to not make things worse. Jesus says to befriend them. If you learn of someone in financial need, Hillel says not to compound the problem while Jesus says to help meet their need.

Hillel's standard is simpler to follow because it simply requires us *not* to do the wrong thing while Christ calls us to take an active role in making their situation better. James would go on to echo these sentiments in his letter, writing that "whoever knows the right thing to do and fails to do it, for him it is sin" (James 4:17).

However, we should not expect the lost to hold to the same standard. As such, treating others the way we would want to be treated will often mean treating them better than they treat us. It is a constantly sacrificial way of life that will, at times, seem impossibly difficult.

But that's how Jesus lived. As he makes clear in the verses that follow, we would be wise to follow suit.

Walk the narrow path

From this point forward, Jesus shifts his focus from teaching his disciples what it means to follow him to encouraging them that, despite the difficulties such a life will entail, it will be worth it in the end. In each of the three examples that follow, Jesus demonstrates that despite the gray areas that seem to exist all around us, there are ultimately just two classifications of people: those who are saved and those who are not.

Yes, people will be at different places along each path, and, at times, it may seem as though someone is right in the middle of the two. But the existence of that spectrum does not change that the two roads never intersect. Fortunately, even those currently on the path to destruction are in no way destined to remain there.

After all, each of us started on the path to destruction before we accepted Jesus' offer of salvation and moved to the narrow road that leads to life.

To that end, Jesus begins by cautioning us to "enter by the narrow gate. For the gate is wide and the way is easy that leads to destruction, and those who enter by it are many. For the gate is narrow and the way is hard that leads to life, and those who find it are few" (Matthew 7:13–14).

Stenes, the word used in verse 13 to describe the narrow gate, would have conjured up images of small alleys and tight crevices between two rocks. The idea was that it was large enough to fit through but too small to carry much with you or to travel in a large group. The word for the narrow path in verse 14—*tethlimmene*—is similar but with the added dimension of something being compressed, like grain being ground into flour.

By contrast, the word used for the wide gates—*plateia*—was the complete opposite. That word would have brought to mind something like the main gate leading into Jerusalem. Gates such as these were large enough to accommodate a king and his army or herdsmen as they brought their flocks to market. The road associated with the wide path carries a similar connotation. It too is so broad and easy to maneuver through that many walk it without giving their path a second thought.

The only logical reason to choose the narrow gate when presented with both is if you know the destination at the end will be worth it. And while Jesus promises that it is, he also indicates that the path itself serves an important function.

While the wide gate and broad road were designed to make things as easy and appealing to as many people as possible, the small gate and narrow path were designed to challenge people, and, through the resulting pressure, help them become more like Christ.

Most of us have two people we are capable of being at any given point in time: the person who is easy to be and the person God wants us to be. We are incapable of becoming the latter in our own power, though. The only way to consistently walk along the narrow path is to do so in God's strength rather than our own. That said, it does get easier over time as following Christ's example begins to feel more natural the more often we do it. That doesn't mean it will ever be easy or that the broad path won't seem appealing from time to time, but it also doesn't have to feel like a perpetual struggle.

Even as we make the conscious effort to remain on the narrow path to life, though, obstacles and temptations can beckon us back to the easy road. And when that call comes from those who claim to follow Christ as well, resisting it can be even more difficult.

False prophets

False prophets had been an issue since the time of Moses and were among God's greatest enemies during the time of Jeremiah and the other true prophets (Deuteronomy 18:20; Jeremiah 31:30–32). Jesus also warned against them repeatedly throughout his ministry, as we see in passages such as this one and Matthew 24:24. The heroes of the Early Church would also deal with them on a repeated basis (Acts 13:6–12; 2 Corinthians 11:13–15; 1 John 4:1–3; 2 Peter 2:1–3).

However, not all false prophets are bad people. What can make them particularly troublesome is that they often spread lies without intending to do so.

During the time of the prophets, for example, those who opposed God's word usually did so because their hearts and minds were set on things other than the Lord. And during the time of Christ, the error of the religious leaders—the primary targets of Jesus' rebuke in this passage—was much the same.

As discussed in chapter 2, many of those who attempted to disrupt Christ's ministry and emphasized the need to obey a legalistic understanding of God's word did so because they thought that was the best way to bring people into communion with the Lord. They were wrong, of course, but understanding that someone can be a false prophet without intending to be is crucial for recognizing them when they appear.

It's also necessary to understand that the outward appearance of such people will often look exactly like it should. They may appear to be pious and devout followers of Christ, but the old saying "wolves in sheep's clothing" exists for a reason. All of us have experienced, at one time or another, people who appeared to be someone that their actions would later reveal to be a lie. Such is the case with false prophets.

As such, Eugene Peterson translates this verse well: "Don't be impressed with charisma; look for character" (Matthew 7:15, MSG). Many who fall from the narrow path are enticed to do so because they valued the former more than the latter.

Fortunately, a clear path exists to recognize the deception of false prophets.

Fruit inspectors

As Jesus notes, false prophets can be recognized "by their fruits," adding, "Are grapes gathered from thornbushes, or figs from thistles? So, every healthy tree bears good fruit, but the diseased tree bears bad fruit" (Matthew 7:16–17).

True followers of Christ will tend to act like Christ. That doesn't mean we will be perfect all the time, but, when people look at our lives, they should see Jesus' influence coming through.

However, there is a reason this instruction came after his words against judgment at the start of Matthew 7. The temptation to take Christ's words in this passage as a license to pass judgment on any whose lives do not appear to bear good fruit must be tempered by the warning that, in general, we are not great at judging others fairly. As such, discerning true believers from false prophets by their actions requires that we are fully reliant on the Holy Spirit to guide that process.

All of us make mistakes, and if we start looking for bad fruit then that's what we're likely to notice most. If we're not careful, our well-placed fear of false prophets can result in us finding them wherever we look. Christ's call in these verses is to discernment rather than fault-finding, and we must be sure that our efforts reflect that purpose.

At the same time, if Jesus' guidance is intended solely to help believers recognize false prophets, then why would the warning in verse 19 be necessary? After all, the caution that "every tree that does not bear good fruit is cut down and thrown in the fire" would, on the surface, appear unnecessary for Christ's disciples. Two possible reasons come to mind.

First, even if Christians do not need to fear that consuming fire, it is important to remember that it remains the fate for those who reject Christ's offer of salvation. If we become complacent in the knowledge that we are not part of the thistles, then we will fail to live out God's purpose for our lives.

The only Christ most people will know is the one they see in us, and it is our responsibility to make sure that when they look at us, they see him. The idea that any should face what awaits those who do not bear good fruit should both horrify and frighten us, and we are more likely to produce good fruit when we share God's concern for their eternal fate.

The second reason for this word of caution is that Jesus' words should serve as a warning to those who think themselves Christians but whose lives do not testify to that claim.

As our culture becomes increasingly accepting of the decision to reject religion—and Christianity in particular—there will perhaps be fewer people who go to church on Sundays and claim to follow Jesus because it's simply the acceptable thing to do. Still, it would be naïve to think that everyone with whom we worship on Sunday morning is going to heaven. Odds are that there are some in our communities of faith who think themselves saved but who lack a personal relationship with Jesus.

More will be said about those who fall into this category in a moment, but Christ's warning serves as an important reminder that claiming to be part of the good fruit tree when nothing but thorns and thistles are evident in your life should be a wake-up call to any who wrongly consider themselves disciples of Jesus. The religious leaders who rejected Jesus in their pursuit of serving God fit this description well. And people can be just as susceptible to that mistake today.

Claiming "Lord, Lord"

From the warning about good and bad fruit, Jesus moves quickly to a less figurative example of the same basic principle. Eugene Peterson's translation once again captures the essence of Christ's words well: "Knowing the correct password—saying 'Master, Master,' for instance—isn't going to get you anywhere with me" (Matthew 7:21, MSG).

Peterson's translation is helpful in that it clearly captures the fundamental difference between knowing *about* Christ and *knowing* Christ. As mentioned in the previous section, many in the first century and many today fail to mark that distinction, and their eternity hangs in the balance.

The ancient understanding of illness was often centered on the belief that it was the result of demons or other dark forces. Thus, if you were able to help someone overcome their sickness, chances were good that it would be seen as a miracle.

The result was that it was quite possible for people to perform what would have seemed like miraculous works without needing divine authority to do so. Early church leaders never denied the existence of these kinds of miracles, and those in question would get the glory for the miracle whether or not God's hand had been the source of the healing.

It seems like this sort of "healer" is who Jesus calls into question in this passage. If that is the case, then what Jesus is essentially saying is that he wasn't fooled. They may have said the right things and even performed some seemingly miraculous signs, but those were not proof of a relationship with him.

Peterson paraphrases Christ's response to such people well: "And do you know what I am going to say? 'You missed the boat. All you did was use me to make yourselves important. You don't impress me one bit. You're out of here'" (Matthew 7:23, MSG).

Note that Jesus isn't saying that it was wrong of these people to prophesy, drive out demons, or perform miracles. The problem was that these good works were done for their glory rather than God's, to make them seem important rather than the Lord. As with those who prayed, fasted, or gave in order to win the praise of people, they have received their reward in full.

You see, it's not enough to simply act the part of a faithful disciple. There has to be substance to it and a personal relationship as the foundation.

However, if you read this text and are concerned that it might be talking about you, then chances are good that it's not. That's not a guarantee, as it could be that God is using these verses to alert you to the fact that you do fall among those who have served the Lord without having a personal relationship with him. But it's important to remember that the people about whom Jesus speaks in this passage were genuinely surprised when he rejected them. It had never occurred to them that they might not be saved because they were certain that their good works were enough to merit that salvation.

Those who have placed their faith in Christ have every reason to feel confident in their eternal fate, but because true salvation is an act of faith and comes from the awareness that there is nothing we could possibly do to earn it, it's understandable if we have moments of doubt. After all, the idea that the God of the universe would become human and die on our behalf so that, through nothing more than faith, we could enter into eternal life with him is pretty unbelievable.

It just also happens to be true.

Our assurance is not based on our words or our works but on Christ's. If you have asked him to be your Lord and Savior, to forgive your sins, and are committed to living as his disciple, then you can rest easy in that assurance. And if you're not sure, now is the perfect time to make that decision.

As Jesus warns in the final passage of his sermon, storms are coming, and knowing that your soul is secure in him is the only way to weather them well.

Firm foundations

Jesus concludes his sermon with the promise that everyone "who hears these words of mine and does them will be like a wise man who built his house on the rock. And the rain fell, and the floods came, and the winds blew and beat on that house, but it did not fall, because it had been founded on the rock" (Matthew 7:24–25).

However, he also promises that "everyone who hears these words of mine and does not do them will be like a foolish man who built his house on the sand. And the rain fell, and the floods came, and the winds blew and beat against that house, and it fell, and great was the fall of it" (Matthew 7:26–27).

The rock—*petra* in Greek—to which Jesus refers in this passage is the layer of limestone that was found beneath the topsoil throughout this region of Galilee. You were all but guaranteed to find it if you were willing to dig deep enough. When carpenters would start building a house, one of the first things they would do is dig until they found this firm foundation and then begin their construction.

By contrast, the sand to which the rock is compared referred to the topsoil and loose rock that lies on top of the *petra*. The person who builds their house on the sand had every opportunity to dig a little deeper and find rock. That their house lacks a firm foundation is a choice rather than due to circumstances beyond their control. And they won't discover the full cost of their mistake until it's too late.

This short parable illustrates a few very important truths.

The first is that the rains, floods, and raging winds that batter both houses are not questions of *if* they will happen but rather *when* they will happen. Jesus was clear that "in the world you will have tribulation" (John 16:33). Sometimes that trouble will be of your own doing and sometimes it won't.

Either way, acting surprised, dismayed, or accusatory when the storms come will not lessen the threat they pose. The only question that really matters is this: When the storms rage, will you be left standing after they pass?

If our lives are firmly planted on God, we will be.

That said, surviving the storm doesn't mean going through it unscathed, which leads to the second truth we learn from this parable.

One of the most difficult aspects of the trials we face in life is that our faith will not always preserve us like we think it should. It's all right to experience moments of doubt or feel overwhelmed in the midst of the storm. After all, why would God say that he was the great comforter if there were never the need for us to be comforted (Isaiah 51:12)? The Lord can only comfort those who are willing to receive it, though. If we cling to our doubts and anger rather than taking them to the Lord, trading them for his peace and understanding, then our homes will be left with a lot more cracks once the storm passes.

Revealing those cracks is often part of God's redemption. This side of heaven, none of us will ever have a perfect relationship with the Lord. Our faith will always be stronger in some areas than others, and helping us see where our house may have shifted from its foundation is one of the most important purposes of the storms.

The third truth we learn from this parable is that it is crucial for every aspect of our lives to be based on the firm foundation of God's word. In the Sermon on the Mount, Jesus offers a holistic view of what a Christian's life should look like. The reality is, though, some facets of those teachings come more naturally to us than others. The temptation we must resist is to think that we can ever excel at those parts to the point that it compensates for the places where our faithfulness to Christ's words is less consistent.

Jesus is clear in these verses that any aspects of our lives built on sand will be swept away by the storms. How much better, then, would it be if we allowed God to show us where we're slipping from his word before circumstances make those faults abundantly clear?

Conclusion

Jesus came that we "may have life and have it abundantly" (John 10:10).

There will always be those who try to find it on their own or by taking what appears to be an easier path. They may even do so while claiming to be Christians.

However, abiding in the entirety of God's word and relying upon the foundation he provides is the only way to experience that abundant life.

Will you?

8

Recognize God's authority

Matthew 7:28–29

(Astonished crowds)

Matthew's account of the Sermon on the Mount ends with the simple statement that "when Jesus finished these sayings, the crowds were astonished at his teaching, for he was teaching them as one who had authority, and not as their scribes" (Matthew 7:28–29).

The Greek word translated here as "astonished" more literally means to be beside yourself with amazement or to be spellbound. The reason for their astonishment is even more important than the reaction itself, though. They were amazed by the authority with which Jesus taught.

Authority is a concept most of us understand, at least on some level. Chances are good that you either have a boss or have worked under a boss at some point in your career.

If you're in school, you understand what it's like to sit under a teacher's authority and learn from them. The term used in Matthew's gospel, however, implies far more than simply being in a position of power. Its more literal meaning is "out of your own being," and it was an entirely new way of teaching in the first century.

Twelve times in this sermon, Jesus stated, "I say unto you." No rabbi had ever spoken that way because to do so intimated that you had the authority to interpret the Scriptures for yourself, and that was simply not done. Rabbis in Jesus' day would quote previous rabbis quoting previous rabbis and so on, until the lineage of thought lost its source.

In a sense, that hesitancy is admirable. After all, much of Christ's Sermon on the Mount was spent correcting the many mistakes that still filtered into their teachings despite the claim to have no authority to offer their own interpretation of God's word. They were right to fear the kind of authority Jesus exhibited freely. But their unwillingness to take that step themselves was a large part of why Christ's authority had such a profound effect on the crowds.

Jesus, as the Son of God and author of the Scriptures, spoke with greater authority than the scribes and religious leaders because he possessed a greater authority. The religious leaders were afraid to speak with authority because they implicitly understood they didn't have it. Jesus could because he did. And, given the nature of the life to which he was calling them, establishing that authority was a necessary precursor to their obedience.

What was true for them is true for us as well.

If we are going to not only accept Christ's words but also put them into practice, then we have to recognize the authority with which they were spoken. The Sermon on the Mount was essentially Christ's attempt to reset the way people related to God.

Given that many in our culture—including many Christians—prefer a brand of spirituality that allows them to pick and choose the parts they like while ignoring the parts they don't, recognizing that Jesus definitively refused to give us that option can be a tough truth to accept.

Were these words the mere suggestion of a pastor or friend, they could be ignored. But, when coming from the mouth of incarnate God, they become infinitely more difficult to push aside.

Hear the Sermon for the first time

In a moment, we will conclude our discussion on the Sermon on the Mount by reading or listening to Christ's words in their entirety.

But before we do, take a few minutes to reflect on what it means to hear commands spoken with the authority of God himself.

How committed are you to living out every facet of his teachings today?

Are there any parts of your life in which you've been convicted over the course of this book?

When was the last time you were truly astonished by God?

When you're ready:

- Pull out your Bible or find an audio version to listen to. Then go through the Sermon in its entirety.

- Ignore the chapter breaks and subheadings to simply take in Christ's words as if you were listening to them for the first time.

- When you're done, take a few moments to sit and reflect on whatever the Lord might want to teach you from his word.

Christ's standards for his disciples have not changed over the centuries since this Sermon was first delivered.

What he expected of his followers on that hillside are still his expectations for us today.

How we respond to those expectations each day determines whether we will survive the storms or be washed away.

How solid is your foundation?

Appendix: A brief summary of the Beatitudes

While more is said about each of the Beatitudes in our book *Blessed: Eight Ways Christians Change Culture*, below is a brief summary of the characteristics described in Matthew 5.

1. "Blessed are the poor in spirit, for theirs is the kingdom of heaven" (v. 3): We begin every day by submitting to the Holy Spirit, seeking his empowering and leading through our life and service.

2. "Blessed are those who mourn, for they shall be comforted" (v. 4): We stand with those who suffer, showing God's love in our compassion.

3. "Blessed are the meek, for they shall inherit the earth" (v. 5): We submit daily to God's control, trusting him to use our gifts and opportunities to advance his kingdom.

4. "Blessed are those who hunger and thirst for righteousness, for they shall be satisfied" (v. 6): We seek to be people of personal integrity so the Spirit can use us and others will see Christ in us.

5. "Blessed are the merciful, for they shall receive mercy" (v. 7): As an example of God's grace, we choose to pardon those who have hurt us.

6. "Blessed are the pure in heart, for they shall see God" (v. 8): We live for the singular purpose of loving God and others with passion and joy.

7. "Blessed are the peacemakers, for they shall be called sons of God" (v. 9): We choose to be at peace with God, others, and ourselves so as to offer God's peace to our fallen world.

8. "Blessed are those who are persecuted for righteousness' sake, for theirs is the kingdom of heaven" (v. 10): We face the opposition of our culture with courage and joy.

Each of these qualities is essential to becoming the kind of people God created us to be. Each is also essential to the kind of character required to live out the commands Jesus gives in the remainder of the Sermon on the Mount.

Many people think Jesus' teachings here are unattainable—an impractical, idealized goal. And they rightly recognize it would be impossible to live up to the standards Christ imparts in their own strength.

Fortunately, Jesus recognized that fact as well, which is why he began by outlining the kind of character that will make the rest of the Sermon on the Mount possible. While God knows we cannot practice them perfectly, he commands that we try. And he promises that, when we do, we will experience a kind of blessing that can only come from him.

About the Authors

RYAN DENISON, PHD, is the Senior Editor for Theology at Denison Forum. He consults on *The Daily Article* and provides writing and research for many of the ministry's productions.

He earned his PhD in church history at BH Carroll Theological Institute after having received his MDiv at Truett Seminary. Ryan has also taught at BH Carroll and Dallas Baptist University. He and his wife, Candice, live in East Texas and have two children.

JIM DENISON, PHD, is a cultural theologian and the founder and CEO of Denison Ministries. Dallas-based Denison Ministries includes DenisonForum.org, First15.org, ChristianParenting.org, and FoundationsWithJanet.org. Dr. Denison speaks biblically into significant cultural issues at DenisonForum.org and DrJimDenison.com, as well as on radio, TV, podcasts, and social media. He is the author of over 30 books and has taught the philosophy of religion and apologetics at several seminaries. He holds a Doctor of Philosophy and a Master of Divinity degree from Southwestern Baptist Theological Seminary. He also received an honorary Doctor of Divinity from Dallas Baptist University. Prior to launching Denison Forum in 2009, he pastored churches in Texas and Georgia. Jim and his wife, Janet, live in Dallas, Texas. They have two married sons and four grandchildren.

About Denison Ministries

DENISON MINISTRIES is a Christian nonprofit where meaningful content transforms lives. And transformed lives transform the world around them.

Denison Ministries includes four brands: DenisonForum.org, ChristianParenting.org, First15.org, and FoundationsWithJanet.org.